BLUE

BY
Michael Hainey

FEATURING

Blueprints
the Blue Sky
Blue Sky Laws
the Deep Blue Sea
Blue Whales
Blue Tongued Skinks
Bluenoses
Blue Plate Specials
Blue Diamonds
the Blues
Blue Ribbons
Blue Moons
Blue Light Specials
Blue Screens
Blue Jeans
and Much More!

1 2 3 4 5 6 7 8 9 -GC- 0100999897

First printing, September 1997

Through the Addison Wesley Longman TRI▲NGLE Program, Planet Dexter books are available FROM YOUR BOOKSELLER at special discounts for bulk purchases; or, contact the Corporate, Government, and Special Sales Department at Addison Wesley Longman, One Jacob Way, Reading, MA 01867, or call (800) 238-9682.

AND NOW A MESSAGE FROM OUR BLUE-BLOODED CORPORATE LAWYER:

"Neither the Publisher nor the Author shall be liable for any damage that may be caused or sustained as a result of conducting any of the activities in this book without specifically following instructions, conducting the activities without proper supervision, or ignoring the cautions contained in the book."

THE PLANET DEXTER GUARANTEE!

If for any reason you're not satisfied with this book, please send a simple note telling us why (how else will we be able to make our future books better?!) along with the book to:
The Editors of Planet Dexter, One Jacob Way, Reading, MA 01867-3999

We'll read your note carefully, and send back to you a free copy of another Planet Dexter book. And we'll keep doing that until we find the perfect Planet Dexter book for you.

COOL, EH?

ILLUMINATINGLY WRITTEN BY

Michael **Blue** Hainey

PROJECT MANAGEMENT BY

MKR **Fluorescent** Design inc.

OPALINE ART DIRECTION BY

Marta **Sapphire** Ruliffson

IRIDESCENT COVER DESIGN BY

C. Shane **Azure** Sykes

INTERIOR DESIGN & ILLUSTRATIONS BY

Robert **Cobalt** Brook Allen

WATERCOLOR FLOWERS BY

Leslie **Periwinkle** Watkins

EDITORIAL RESEARCH BY

Rosie **Violet** Amodio

Welcome to the Blue Book

THE BOOK THAT'S YOUR TRUE-BLUE❈ FRIEND

What's a blue book? you ask. Well, it's a look at the world of . . . blue. (You thought we were kidding, didn't you?)

But *Blue* is also a book unlike any other book. We could go on and on and tell you just why that is—we could go on and on, in fact, until we're blue in the face, but then you'd say we blue you away. And we don't want to do that. Because then you wouldn't read the book.

So, instead of us telling you about *Blue*, we think you would have a lot more fun if we blue out of here and let you read all the un-blue-lieveable things we've discovered for you and put in this one *Blue* book.

❈(By the way, the term "true blue" dates back to the 1600s. England, led by Charles I, and Scotland were on the verge of civil war. To fight the English, the Scottish clans united and swore loyalty to each other. As a sign of their loyalty, they went into battle as one army under a blue banner. Thus, they said they'd be "true blue.")

A TIP: If you don't like anything in this book, circle it with a blue pencil. That's what a book editor does. When someone writes a book, an editor reads it (like your teacher reads your reports) and, using a blue pencil, circles things that should be corrected or taken out.

We hope of course you like everything in this book!

3

A.K.A. THE TABLE OF CONTENTS

Most books have a table of contents that tells you where you'll find each part of the story. But since this is *Blue*, we're using a blueprint instead.

A blueprint is a copy of the original drawing that shows the instructions for how to make something. Before anything large and complicated gets created (like a house, an airplane, a computer, or even this book), the people who are manufacturing it make a drawing of it.

This original drawing is called the "mechanical drawing." But because lots of people will help to build the house or the computer, lots of copies of the drawing are needed. These copies of the original mechanical drawing are "blueprints." Trying to create something without a blueprint is like trying to take a long journey without ever looking at a road map: you'll probably get lost.

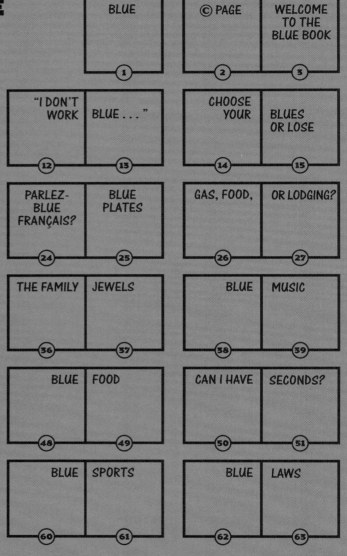
PLANET DEXTER

64 PAGES

BLUE

TABLE OF CONTENTS

ISBN 0-201-87396-6

THE BLUEPRINT

So why are blueprints blue?

Well, blueprints were invented by an Austrian monk in the 1800s. To make a blueprint, the original drawing is done on a thin paper. This drawing is then placed on special blueprint paper and coated with a kind of salt. Then, these papers are exposed to a bright light. What happens next is sort of like a photograph. The special paper underneath the original turns to two colors: blue and white. It turns to white where pencil lines prevented light from reaching the paper. Where there were no pencil lines to block out the light, the paper turns to blue (Turnbull's blue, to be exact).

OFF WE GO...

Into the Wild Blue Yonder

Okay, so just what is blue? Good question. And now that we have your attention, we'll tell you.

The Blue See. See. See?

Blue is one of three primary colors. (Quick! Can you name the other two? Give up? The other two are red and yellow.) Of all the colors in the world, the primary colors are the most pure because they cannot be made by mixing colors together. All other colors are made from these three colors.

For instance:
BLUE + YELLOW = GREEN
BLUE + RED = PURPLE

So were it not for blue, you wouldn't have many of the colors in the world. And were it not for blue, you wouldn't have this book, either. (Hey, isn't the world a great place?)

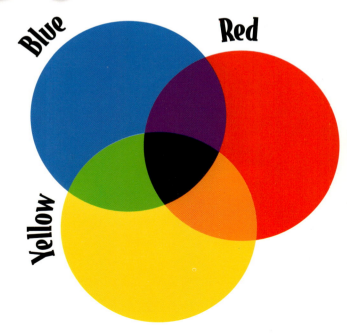

Blue

Red

Yellow

What to Call Blue

IF YOU WANNA BE PICKY ABOUT IT

How many shades of blue are there? Believe it or not, the United States government, through its Department of Commerce, actually keeps track of all the different names for shades of blue (like midnight blue, or navy blue) with the Universal Color Language. It was created so that scientists, teachers, artists, and business people can be sure that when they talk about midnight blue, they are all referring to the same shade. In other words, it's the dictionary of color, since it defines what each shade looks like.

Blue or False?

This page contains 11 names for shades of blue. Six of them are real shades of blue as named by the Universal Color Language, but five of them are names we made up. Can you spot the true blues?

- ☐ Light Blue
- ☐ Midnight Blue
- ☐ Bavarian Blue
- ☐ Wavy Blue
- ☐ Indistop Blue
- ☐ Navy Blue
- ☐ Indigo Blue
- ☐ New Reduced Calorie and Low Fat Blue
- ☐ He-Who-Accuses Blue
- ☐ Periwinkle Blue
- ☐ The Fuses Blue

ANSWERS: the true-blue names are Indigo, Midnight, Bavarian, Navy, Periwinkle, Light Blue

A Blue by Any Other Name?

Hey, what's to stop you from inventing a new shade of blue? So put on your thinking cap and start with a name. What would you call the blue that you invent?

Write the name here

Now all you need to do is invent it, then give those pinheads at the Department of Commerce a call. Go to it!

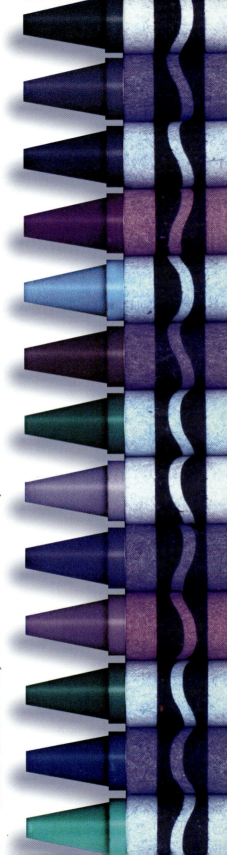

COLOR ME BLUE According to Crayola Crayons, kids' two most favorite crayon colors are blue and red. And did you know that the crayon called "midnight blue" was originally called "Prussian blue"? Crayola changed the name because they didn't think anyone knew what a Prussian was. Well, do you? (Prussia is what Germany was once named. Its soldiers wore uniforms that were a deep blue. That was Prussian blue.)

LOOK UP!

OR, WHY IS THE SKY BLUE?

Speaking of the Wild Blue Yonder (that's what lots of people, especially the people in the United States Air Force, call the sky), let's get one big question out of the way right now: Why is the sky blue?

Well, hold on and we'll give you the best, fastest introduction to color, and why we see it, that you'll ever get.

The First Thing you need to know is that, generally speaking, sunlight is white. So why isn't the sky white? Well, it's not white because between the time the sunlight leaves the sun and the time it hits us in the eye, something happens to it. That something is this: it passes through the Earth's atmosphere.

The Second Thing you need to know: white sunlight is actually made up of waves of color. Some of these waves are visible to us and some are not. The waves we can see make up the "visible spectrum." We can see these waves of color when we shine light through a prism. The visible spectrum is made up of the waves we see as red, orange, yellow, green, blue, indigo, and violet. These colors are present in the white sunlight all the time, we just can't always see them.

10

This Area for Sale

BLUE-SKY LAWS

What's that? A law against blue skies? Nope. Blue-sky laws are laws that protect you from being cheated, or buying something that's "so many feet of blue sky." (In other words, nothing. Zip. Zilch. Nada. Because you can't take possession of the sky.) Blue-sky laws makes scams illegal.

The Third Thing you need to know is that when the white sunlight passes through the atmosphere on its way through the sky down to our eyes, it gets broken up and scattered by molecules of dust and water in the sky. Because they are shorter, the blue lightwaves in the sunlight are affected by this and become visible. The other color lightwaves are longer and therefore remain unaffected and invisible. Simple, huh?

Feel smart? You should. That's a lot of science you just learned. It took people thousands of years to figure out the answer to that question, and you learned it in just two minutes. Nice job.

THE WILD BLU-FORD YONDER Former Air Force pilot Guion Stewart Bluford Jr. is America's first African-American astronaut. He flew on the *Challenger Space Shuttle* in 1983. Guion, who was born in 1942, went on to make three more trips on the *Shuttle*. He flew on the *Challenger* again in 1985, then flew on the *Discovery Space Shuttle* in 1991 and in 1992. He has spent 688 hours in space.

1. Elvis Presley
A. recorded an album called *Blue Hawaii*
B. recorded the song, "I Love Eating Blueberry Pies (under Mississippi Skies)"
C. wore blue contact lenses

2. Fats Domino
A. wrote the opera *The Thin Blue Line*
B. sang "Blueberry Hill"
C. starred in the scary movie *The House on Blueberry Hill*

3. Marc Chagall
A. founded the famous rock band Bluedog
B. wrote a collection of poems titled *Electric Blue*
C. created blue stained-glass windows

"I Don't Work

WELL, OKAY, SOMETIMES I DO."

Artists love blue. Pablo Picasso, one of the greatest artists of the twentieth century, loved it so much that he spent the years from 1901 to 1904 making paintings that used only different shades of blue. That's why it's called his Blue Period (sometimes critics can be so creative with titles). But even though he went through a blue period, it wasn't depressing. He went on to make a lot of the green stuff (money) selling his blue paintings.

Artist Vincent van Gogh also had a blue period. But he was depressed. In fact he was so depressed that he cut off his ear.

Yep, blue sure is beautiful. It's only natural that it has inspired various artists to some of their best work. See if you can pass our Blue Artists quiz.

4. Blue Man Group

A. is the name of the New York Police Department's barbershop quartet

B. is the title of a painting by Michelangelo

C. is the name of a theater group

Blue...

5. Gainsborough

A. painted *Blue Boy*

B. wrote the poem "Little Boy Blue"

C. invented blue dog food

6. Vincent Van Gogh

A. created the ballet *White Swan, Blue Lake*

B. painted Starry Night

C. was a color-blind painter of the fifteenth century

COMPOSITION IN RED, WHITE, AND PUKE

Piet Mondrian was a famous twentieth-century painter. He liked to paint with blue, too. He painted blue, red, and yellow squares. Many of his paintings hang in New York's Museum of Modern Art. In 1996, a man named Jubal Brown was at the museum looking at Mondrian's painting, *Composition in Red, White and Blue*. He looked at it, and then he deliberately threw up on it. What was really weird was that his vomit was blue! It's true. Mr. Brown had just eaten blueberry yogurt. The museum quickly cleaned the painting and prevented any damage to it. Mr. Brown later said he vomited on the painting as an "artistic statement" about art he did not like. He planned to puke in the three primary colors, and had already spewed red vomit on a work by the French Impressionist Raoul Dufy.

Choose Your Blues or Lose

TIME FOR YOU TO EXERCISE SOME TASTE

So, now that you know about artists and their love of blue, what's your favorite blue? This page contains 34 shades of blue. Vote for your favorites!

BLUE RULES By the way, did you know that blue is America's favorite color? It's true. In a recent poll, 35 percent of Americans said it was their favorite color. (Green was second with 16 percent and purple was third with 10 percent.) Is blue your favorite color? We sure hope so. Otherwise, you might not be liking this book so much.

Oh Say Can You See....

the Blue Sea?

Or, Why the Sea Isn't Orange

Wait a minute! How come sometimes oceans or lakes look blue and other times they look green? Just what color is water anyway? Good question. And have we got a good answer for you.

THE REALLY, REALLY DEEP BLUE SEA

The deepest known point on the Earth's surface is the Mariana Trench. It's a valley on the floor of the north Pacific Ocean, about two hundred miles east of the Mariana Islands (can you find them on a map?). It's 35,820 feet (about 7 miles) from the surface of the ocean, to the bottom of the trench; the trench is 1,580

H.R.M.S. TITANIC

The ocean is blue for the same reason the sky is blue: The blue light in the spectrum is scattered by the water molecules; the other colors pass through the water, so we don't see them.

Sometimes the ocean looks green because there's a lot of algae in the water.

HAVE AN ICE TIME

Water freezes, of course. And really big pieces of frozen water are glaciers and icebergs. (Watch out for those if you're in a ship! The H.R.M.S. *Titanic* hit an iceberg in 1912 and sank in the Atlantic Ocean. The *Titanic* was supposed to be "unsinkable.") Glaciers and icebergs aren't white—they're blue. It's all because of (you guessed it) how light gets filtered through them.

miles long. It was probably made by volcanic activity and the shifting of the Earth's surface. In 1960, American Don Walsh and Frenchman Jacques Picard descended to 35,800 feet and explored the trench from inside their bathyscaphe, *Trieste*. (In case you were wondering, a bathyscaphe is a special ship, sort of like a tiny submarine, that is used to explore the deep seas. Unlike a submarine, a bathyscaphe moves like a ship in the water.)

The Seven, Six.... Three! Seas

Since ancient times, people have talked about the oceans as the "Seven Seas."

But modern day oceanographers (they're the people who study the deep blue sea) now divide the ocean into just three oceans: Atlantic, Pacific, Indian.

Hey, we hate to sound so smart, but if you want to get really official, there's really just one global ocean. When you get down to it, it's all a single big mass of water that just keeps sloshing from one place to the next.

BIG BLUE

More than 70 percent of the Earth is covered with water. (That's why Earth has the nickname "Big Blue"—because from space, where Guion Bluford has been, Earth looks like a big blue marble.)

18

Seven Up

Are you a smooth sailor or a leaky dinghy? In the list below are the original Seven Seas that ancient sailors talked about. Circle the anchor in front of the real names.

1. the Mediterranean
2. the Sea Saw
3. the Deep Blue Sea
4. the Red Sea
5. the East African Sea
6. the West African Sea
7. the Emergen Sea
8. the Cold Sea
9. the China Sea
10. the Persian Gulf,
11. the Sea-U-Later
12. the Indian Ocean
13. the Sea NB Seen

ANSWERS: 1, 4, 5, 6, 9, 10, 12 are the real seas.

Hello, My Name is...

S o, now that you know the sea names, we should also tell you that it was not until 1845 that the names Atantic, Pacific, and Indian were accepted by everyone in the world as the official names of the three oceans. Before that, the Atlantic and the Pacific had different names. Can you match the old name with the new name?

Old Name	New Name
1. Atlantic	**A.** Western Ocean
2. Pacific	**B.** Great Ocean

WE'VE CLEARED THAT UP...
The clearest ocean water is in a northern section of the Atlantic Ocean known as the Sargasso Sea. The water there is not blue; it's as clear as drinking water and you can see down into it for 20 feet.

H.R.M.S. TITANIC

BUT THIS IS AS CLEAR AS...
Did you ever wonder what is at the bottom of the deep blue sea? Well, it's a lot of mud. Not sand, but mud. Mud is the most common sediment on the deep-ocean floor. (As far as we know, there are no mud pie stores down there. And no one has seen any sea monsters, either.)

Blue Beasts

Blue whales are the largest animals that have ever lived. They can get as long as 100 feet and weigh more than 120 tons—as much as 1,500 men combined. (A baby blue whale gains 10 pounds per hour.) They're slate blue, but have no teeth. Instead, they have two plate-like filters made of little hairs, called "baleen." They use these to filter out tiny plankton from the water.

What other blue animals are there? Well . . . "blue" animals are actually more gray than blue. But people like to call the animals blue because it sounds better. Regardless, here is the blue menagerie:

Bluefish are known as the ocean killers. They live primarily in the Atlantic, grow to be about 15 inches long, and are very ferocious. They're also known as "chopping machines," and cut up other fish into little pieces. Former president George Bush has a bluefish bite on his hand. He got it when he caught one fishing and, trying to take it off the hook, got bitten!

Honey blue-eyes are small fish that live off the northern coast of Australia.

Slender **snipefish** are entirely blue. They live in the Mediterranean, the Atlantic, and near Japan. They can swim as fast backward as they can forward. So the next time someone asks you to go snipe hunting, tell them you would much rather go snipe fishing instead.

Bluethroat pikeblenny fish live off the Florida coast. Only the males are blue, and when one male invades the territory of another male, they fight by locking mouths and pushing each other back and forth. Whichever fish can bite the other first is the winner.

Blue tang (no, the astronauts did not eat them on the moon) fish can change color during the course of the day.

Bluegill fish live in many American lakes.

Blue catfish can weigh more than 100 pounds.

Blue parrotfish live in the Atlantic ocean. When they sleep at night, they cover themselves in a slimy substance that they produce (kind of like when you drool all over your pillow at night). These slimy pajamas protect them from nighttime attacks by moray eels.

Blue crabs live off the United States Atlantic coast. They have blue legs.

Bluebottle flies
are those bright, shiny blue flies you often see. Did you know that they breed in rotting flesh? (Cool!)

Band-winged grasshoppers,
which are common in America and Europe, have blue hind wings.

Blue-heads
are worms. Some people use them as bait to catch bluefish.

Blue-tongued skinks
have blue tongues and live in Australia. But skinks are not skunks. They're small lizards.

Blue sheep
live in the mountains of Asia. They are blue only when they're young. They turn gray when they get older.

Blue hares
are a species of hare. They look pure white when they're in the snow, but when they're in the shade, they look bluish. They live primarily near the Arctic Circle, but also in parts of Europe.

Blue foxes
are a species of Arctic fox. They live near (duh) the Arctic Circle. They're rare.

Blue antelopes
are a kind of antelope that live in herds on the African grasslands.

ATTENTION, BATMAN!
Robins aren't blue, but their eggs are.

Bluebirds
are three species of songbirds that live in North America. There's the eastern bluebird, the western bluebird, and the mountain bluebird. And yes, they do bring happiness.

Blue jays
are found throughout North America. They're related to crows.

Great blue herons
live in the southern United States.

HAPPY HUNTING
By the way, the "blue bird of happiness" that people talk about comes from the play by Maurice Maeterlinck called *L'Oiseau Bleu*—that's French for "The Blue Bird"—where people are searching for happiness and happiness is compared to a little blue bird.

Kerry blue terriers
are the national dog of Ireland. They're great at herding, hunting, being watchdogs, or being pets. But their fur is not really blue—it's a deep gray.

Blue heelers
are Australian cattle dogs.

The Blues
make up an entire family of butterflies. Several hundred species belong to it. Most are very small and fragile. Karner Blue butterflies are a very rare insect; with their wings open, they're only the size of a quarter.

Blue People

You see more blue animals than you do blue people. Blue people just don't exist. Unless, of course, they're invented:

like **Genie** from Aladdin or a **Smurf** or Paul Bunyan's buddy, **Babe the Blue Ox**, or Mel Gibson in **Braveheart** or **Bluebeard** (he was a pirate who kept killing his wives so he could marry new ones. Yikes!)

Baby Blues

There are no real blue people but there are some famous blue-eyed folks: like Frank Sinatra or Paul Newman. What blue-eyed people do you know?

Write the names here

Speaking of baby blues, all babies are not born with blue eyes, as is sometimes said to be the case. Their eyes only look blue because they're cloudy (remember, the little baby is opening her eyes to look at the world for the first time). Their real eye color is present, it's just that the pigment—the color in the eye—has not settled.

BLUE BOY

Here's a famous poem, a nursery rhyme you might know. (But no one knows who wrote it):

Little Boy Blue,  come blow your horn.

The sheep's in the meadow,

The cow's in the corn.

Where is the boy who looks after the sheep? He's under a haystack, fast asleep.

Will you wake him? No, not I,

For if I do, he's sure to cry.

Bluenoses and Blue-domers

Ever heard someone called a "bluenose"? The term describes a puritanical person, maybe because of their "frigid" or cold manner (you know how your nose turns blue out in the cold). The Puritans lived in New England, where the cold weather made their noses "blue."

Someone who might not like the bluenoses is a "blue-domer"—that's the word for a person who doesn't believe in going to a formal church but prefers to worship beneath the "blue dome" of the sky.

"Blue nose certificates" used to be given out on British Navy ships when the sailors crossed into the Arctic Circle as proof they made the trip.

Blue Bloods

Some people are called "blue bloods," but humans don't really have blue blood. If you have blue blood, you're a crustacean (like a lobster!)—they're the only animals in the world with blue blood. Freaky! Crustacean blood is blue because it has copper in it, unlike the blood of humans and all other animals, which has iron in it. Human blood is red (except for when it is on its way back to the heart and is lacking in oxygen; then it's sort of deep purple). It's our veins that are blue.

Generally speaking, blue bloods are people who think they are in the upper classes (rich parts) of society. The term comes from Spanish noblemen in the Middle Ages who wanted to say they were better than the Moors, a dark-skinned people from the Middle East who had invaded and ruled Spain. The Spanish said their skin was lighter, and because of this, you could see their blue veins, so they were the blue bloods. The term stuck and now all people of the so-called upper class say they are blue bloods.

Parlez Blue Français?

Here's how to say blue in 28 languages, so you'll be ready wherever you go in the world.

Afrikaans: blou (blow)

Arabic: azrug (az-ROOG)

Belarus: sini (see-NEE)

Croatian: plav (plav)

Czech: blu (bloo)

Danish: blå (bloh)

Farsi: abi (a-BEE)

Finnish: alakuloinen (ah-LAK-oo-loin-en)

French: bleu (bluh)

German: blau (blau)

Greek: blou (blou)

Hebrew: tsava kachol (TSA-vah kai-YOL)

Hungarian: kek (keck)

Indonesian: biru (BEE-roo)

Italian: azzurro (az-ZOOR-row)

Japanese: ao (ow)

Malay: biru (bee-roo)

Mandarin: lan (lan)

Norwegian: blå (blah)

Persian: nílah (NEE-la)

Portugese: azul (ah-ZOOL)

Rumanian: albastru (AL-bas-troo)

Russian: cuhEE (see-nee-YUH)

Spanish: azul (ah-ZOOL)

Swedish: blå (bla)

Swahili: bulu (BOO-loo)

Urdu: azdure (AH-zoor)

Ukrainian: cuhee (SEEH-nee-yuh)

BON VOYAGE! If you take a trip to a foreign country, don't forget your United States passport. If you don't have a passport, a country won't let you enter because they don't know what country you're coming from. It will be easy to remember your passport—the color of it is blue.

HEY, WHERE AM I? And when you go to another country, you might want to bring a guide book so you'll know where to stay and what to see and do. One of the oldest series of guide books is *The Blue Guide*. Strangely, it's published by A & C Black. A & C Black began publishing these books in 1918 and now have guides to more than 60 countries.

Blue Plates

What's Read and Blue and Fast All Over?

In America, when you go traveling on a road trip, you'll see lots of license plates. Can you name the plates that have blue in them?

You'll be naming them for quite a while because only 12 states do not have blue on their official license plates. (Some have blue, but they are on alternate license plates, like Florida's plate that has the Challenger space craft.) Here are the 12 that are blueless:

South Dakota
New Jersey
Delaware
Missouri
Georgia
Florida
Ohio
Indiana
Vermont
Maryland
Oklahoma
New Mexico

BIG BLUE

ARE YOU SURE YOU DIDN'T FORGET SOMETHING? Next time you go on vacation, don't forget to bring your bluey. A "bluey" is a small bag of clothing carried in travel. The word is Australian dialect. It originally referred to the bag that vagabonds tied to the end of a stick in which they kept their clothes and other travel items.

Gas, Food, or Lodging?

What Blue Can Mean to You

On the highway, blue is the official color for general service signs (these are signs that tell you where to find things like restaurants). Other signs are green (directions) and brown (historical markers).

We've collected a few general service signs. Do you know what each sign means?

1.

This sign means

A. Telephones ahead
B. E.T. phone home
C. Caution! Crank calling zone!

2.

This sign means

A. You are entering a no knife zone
B. There's a restaurant up ahead
C. Attention, you are coming to a fork and spoon in the road

3.

This sign means

A. Danger: Slippery roads ahead due to smushed snakes in road
B. Medical facilities ahead
C. Caution: Snake crossing ahead

4.

This sign means

A. Hotels ahead

B. You had *bed*-der slow down

C. You're at the end of your road

5.

This sign means

A. Tourist information ahead

B. Uh-oh! . . . you're really lost

C. You take the "i" road, they'll take the low road

6.

This sign means

A. Pointy tunnel ahead

B. You are entering a witches area

C. Campgrounds ahead

7.

This sign means

A. This highway is brought to you by the letter "H"

B. Helicopter pad in the area

C. Hospital ahead

ANSWERS: 1. a; 2. b; 3. b; 4. a; 5. a; 6. c; 7. c.

27

Blue Mountain, Mississippi

Blue Mountain, Colorado

Blue Mountains, Jamaica

It's a Blue World After All!

Spread It around

Whether you go by plane, train, or automobile, there are lots of blue places to travel to. Really.

And you could start small, with Blue Eye, Arkansas. Only 34 people live in Blue Eye, which makes it the smallest town in Arkansas.

Or you could start big and go to an entire state. Like Kentucky, the Bluegrass State. Or Delaware, the Blue Hen State.

Here are some of the other blue places in the world:

Bleu, Indonesia
Bleu Cap, St. Pierre and Miquelon
Blue, Arizona
Blue Ash, Ohio
Blue Ball, Ohio
Bluebeard's Castle, St. Thomas
Blue Bell, Pennsylvania
Blue Bell Knoll, Utah
Blueberry River, British Columbia
Blue Cliffs, New Zealand
Blue Creek, Idaho
Blue Creek, Utah
Blue Cypress Lake, Florida
Blue Diamond, Kentucky
Blue Diamond, Nevada
Blue Earth, Minnesota
Blue Earth River, Minnesota
Blue Eye, Missouri
Blue Eye, Arkansas
Bluefield, West Virginia
Bluefield, Jamaica
Bluefield, Nicaragua

Blue Stack Mountains, Ireland

To stop in New York—make that Blue York City. It's the Big Apple, which means it's red. But that doesn't mean there aren't a lot of blue things in America's biggest city. There's certainly a lot of blue people: There are 30 people in the Manhattan phone book with the last name Blue. (There's even someone named Bluemoon and someone named Bluerock!) How many Blue people are in your home town? Check the phone book and write the answer here:

_____

There are also 135 businesses in Manhattan with Blue in their name. Everything from Blue Ribbon Sushi to Blue Supermarket to Blue Baron Limousine Service. How many Blue businesses are there in your home town? Check the phone book and write the answer here:

_____

(And if you do get to Manhattan, you'll find the streets aren't paved with gold, but many are paved with bluestones. They're the blue-gray stones that make up many of the old cobblestone streets. They were dug from nearby quarries.)

Bluefish River, Yukon Territory
Blue Hill, Maine
Blue Hill, Nebraska
Bluehill Bay, Maine
Blue Hill Range, Massachusetts
Blue Hills, Connecticut
Blue Hole, Jamaica
Blue Island, Illinois
Blue Island, Saskatchewan
Blue Jacket, Oklahoma
Bluejoint Lake, Oregon
Blue Lagoon National Park, Zambia
Blue Mesa Reservation, Colorado
Bluemont, Virginia
Blue Mound, Illinois
Blue Mound, Texas
Blue Mountain, Nevada
Blue Mountain, Pennsylvania
Blue Mountain Lake, Arkansas
Blue Mountain Lake, New York
Blue Mountain Pass, Oregon
Blue Mountain Peak, Jamaica

Blue Mountains, Oregon-Washington
Blue Mud, Australia
Blue Mud Bay, Australia
Blue Nile, Ethiopia-Sudan
Blue Nose Lake, Northwest Territory
Blue Rapids, Kansas
Blue Ridge, Georgia
Blue Ridge Lake, Georgia
Blue Ridge Mountains, US
Blue Ridge Parkway, North Carolina
Blue Ridge Parkway, Virginia
Blue River, British Columbia
Blue River, Wisconsin
Blue River, Oregon
Blue River, Colorado
Blue Rocks, Nova Scotia
Blue Springs, Missouri
Blue Springs, Nebraska
Blue Stone Lake, West Virginia
Blue Water, New Mexico
Mont Bleus, Zaire

Blue Mountains, Australia

Salute the Blue

When you travel to different countries or different states, you see different flags. Each of the world's 192 countries has a flag. How well do you know the flags of the world? Do you know if blue is the most popular color for flags in the world? Take a look at all the flags and see if you can figure it out.

If you said No, you're right. Red shows up on more flags than any other color; that makes it the most popular flag color in the world. White is second, and blue is third.

30

UNION BLUES

In America, only four states don't have blue in their flag: Alabama, California, Maryland, and New Mexico. By the way, if you like to study flags, you're a vexillologist!

But Don't Boo-hoo for Blue...

because the flag of the entire world, the United Nations flag, is light blue. It was created in 1946 when the United Nations was founded.

RED WHITE AND BLUE

Of course the American flag has all three of the world's most popular flag colors. The American flag was adopted on June 14, 1777, when the Second Continental Congress at Philadelphia passed a resolution that said, "Resolved, that the flag of the United States be thirteen stripes, alternate red and white; that the union be thirteen stars, white in a blue field representing a new constellation." (Did you know that Betsy Ross did not sew the first flag? Betsy was a seamstress in Philadelphia who made pennants for ships during the American Revolution. In 1870, her grandson claimed she had sewn the first flag. Historians, however, have never found any evidence that this story is true.)

Room with a Blue
If you end up living in the White House, be sure and hang out in the Blue Room. It's a fancy-schmancy oval-shaped room on the second floor. Official receptions are held here.

Blue Eyes in the White House
Most U.S. presidents have had blue eyes. As of 1997, 26 of the 41 presidents had blue or blue-gray eyes. First Lady Jackie Kennedy's eyes were brown, but she liked to write on a special shade of blue stationery called Blue Nile.

America the Bluetiful

Obviously, blue is an important part of America. Here's a (very) short history of five hundred years of America, seen through blue eyes.

1492

Chapter One

In 1492, Columbus sails the ocean blue.

A review: Europeans discover America.

1777

Chapter Two

White stars are sewn on a field of blue.

A review: The red, white, and blue is born during the Revolutionary War.

1500   1600   1700

They Blue Their Money

During the American Civil War, the Confederacy issued paper money that was blue. It came to be known as a "blue back" since its backside was blue. Now American money is green and it's known as "greenbacks."

1861
1865

1940s
1990s

Chapter Five

Will everything go ka-blooey?

A review: America invents the nuclear bomb. Russia invents one, too. The Cold War begins, lasts for almost 50 years, then ends. Everybody wins.

Chapter Three

The Blues battle the Grays.

A review: During the Civil War, the North wears blue, the South wears gray.

1900s

Chapter Four

The popularization of the blues.

A review: Musician W.C. Handy brings this traditional African-American music into the mainstream.

1800

1900

Blue Rocks

Now that you've been all over this big blue Earth, isn't it time you got beneath it? We're talking about looking at what makes up big blue: The rocks beneath your feet. Specifically, the blue ones.

Here are the world's precious blue stones:

Sapphires are a dark blue and one of the world's most valuable stones. The best sapphires were discovered in northern India in 1880. Now, most come from Australia.

Amazonites are often used as an ornamental material.

Lapis Lazulis are a very valuable ornamental rock. The best stuff comes from Afghanistan.

Indicolites are a blue form of tourmaline, and are from Brazil, mainly.

Precious stones (which are what people call stones that are valuable, unlike the rocks that are in your driveway— or your head)

Opals are a precious stone. Their name comes from the Sanskrit upala, meaning "precious stone."

Blue topazes are not a very valuable stone, because they're readily available.

Tanzanites are a form of gem that was discovered in Tanzania only in 1967. But it appears that all of them have been mined and tanzanite is now almost as valuable as sapphires.

Blue spinels look a lot like sapphires, but are not as brilliant (that means reflective, not intelligent. C'mon, we all know rocks don't think).

Blue zircons come from Thailand.

Aquamarines come mostly from Brazil.

Turquoise gets its name (probably) because the original people who introduced it to Europe, hundreds of years ago, were Turk traders.

different make-ups, so the way light can pass through them determines the color we see. get their color from the way they (yes, you guessed it) absorb and reflect light. Just like the ocean. But different stones have

The Family Jewels

Let's Hope it Stays in the Museum

Most diamonds have no color. But one of the world's biggest—and most famous—blue gem stones is actually a diamond. It's the Hope Diamond. And because of an impurity, it has a blue tint.

The Hope Diamond was discovered in India and sold to France's King Louis XIV in 1642. Almost as big as a chicken egg, it became known as the "French Blue." But it also seemed to be cursed.

Louis XIV wore it once, then got smallpox. Louis XV wouldn't touch it. Louis XVI wore it all the time. He, of course, got his head cut off in the French Revolution.

The Diamond was stolen after the Revolution and did not show up again until someone tried to sell it in London in 1830. By this time, it had been cut down a bit in size. Henry Hope, a rich banker, bought it and it became known as the Hope Diamond. The Hope Diamond passed through various hands over the next century, with bad luck following it. (Lots of people in the Hope family mysteriously got sick or died.)

Finally, in 1947, a New York jeweler bought it and donated it to the Smithsonian Museum in Washington, D.C., where you can see it today, sitting inside a bullet-proof case.

DIG THIS Diamonds are very rare and are only found in certain parts of the Earth where they were created by geological forces millions of years ago. The ground around the diamonds is a very dark soil, and diamond hunters call it "blue ground."

Sapphires are one of the world's most valuable stones. It only makes sense that the crown of England has blue sapphires on it. In fact, there are 17 blue sapphires on the crown. (But there are 2,868 diamonds. Wow! Better put on your shades.)

BORN TO BE BLUE

Only three months have blue birthstones: MARCH: aquamarine; SEPTEMBER: sapphire; DECEMBER: turquoise.

Dec
Mar
Sep

That's a lot of blue rocks. But what about blue rock? What are we talking about? Music.

Let's start with the original blue music, the blues.

The Blues

The blues are a musical style invented in America by African Americans. The roots of the blues can be found in the work songs slaves sang before the Civil War, especially down in the Mississippi River delta area. Blues music flourished in the south, especially in Mississippi, but it also was very popular in Memphis, Tennessee.

In the blues, people sing about their lives: hard work, heartaches, problems with money. The blues also have a special musical structure. The music is often slow. In terms of the words, the lyrics are broken into three-line stanzas, where the first and second are the same, and the third is different.

One of the most important blues musicians was W.C. Handy. Although blues music had been around for years, he was the first one to write it down and get it published. The first blues song ever published, in 1912, was his "The Memphis Blues."

Blue Music

Been so long since I seen you.
Been so long since I seen you.
Don't know what I'm gonna do.

There are many important and famous blues musicians. Here are some of them and their songs:

B.B. King:
"The Thrill Is Gone"

Gertrude "Ma" Rainey:
"Bo-Weavil Blues"

John Lee Hooker:
"Boogie Chillen"

Robert Johnson:
"Sweet Home Chicago"

Muddy Waters:
"Rolling Stone"

Howlin' Wolf:
"Little Red Rooster"

Bessie Smith:
"Nobody Knows You When You're Down and Out"

Rock and Roll

Blues music is the foundation of rock and roll. Blues gave rock music much of its sound and subjects. There's even a famous song that says, "The blues had a baby, and they called it rock and roll."

One of the first big rock songs was "Blue Suede Shoes," recorded in 1956. It was written by Carl Perkins and later recorded by Elvis Presley. It also was the first song to become #1 on the rock charts, the country charts, and the rhythm and blues charts.

It made Carl famous, but to this day it also gives him some problems. "All my fans want to step on my shoes," he says. "When I do tours, my feet get terribly sore."

Elvis Presley also sang the song "Blue Hawaii." If you've ever been to his house, Graceland, you might think from all the blue rooms that blue was one of his favorite colors. It wasn't. Elvis liked red. Most of Graceland's rooms used to be red, but after he died, they were repainted blue.

"Blue moon of Kentucky keep on shinin'. Shine on the one who's gone and left me blue."

Bluegrass

Bluegrass is a variety of country music. It was invented by Bill Monroe and his band, the Blue Grass Boys, in the Appalachian Mountain region during the 1950s, and was based in western Kentucky (the bluegrass state). Blue Grass is different from country music because it doesn't use any electric instruments. But it does use electric microphones—which is good, since the singing in bluegrass is high-pitched.

Bill Monroe's most famous song was "Blue Moon of Kentucky." Elvis Presley recorded this song, too.

BLUE RIBBONS If you make a CD of songs that a lot of people buy, you could get a multi-platinum record—which means you've sold two million records. A multi-platinum record is kind of like a blue ribbon: It's the best you can do. How come blue ribbons always go to the first-place winner? Why isn't it green or red? The answer probably goes back to the 1300s when England's King Edward III established the highest honor the crown can give: the Most Noble Order of the Garter. This is a dark blue velvet ribbon that's worn below the left knee. Since then, a "blue ribbon" has always meant "number one."

Singing the Blues

"**A**lice Blue Gown" is the title of a famous waltz from the musical *Irene*. It was written in 1919 and was influenced by that year's popularity of light blue clothes for women. At the time, Alice Roosevelt Longworth (Theodore Roosevelt's daughter) was probably the most famous light-blue dresser, so the song was named for her.

No matter what music you like, here are some other "blue" songs and some bands that sang them:

Am I BLUE?, Billie Holiday; Behind BLUE Eyes, The Who; Between the Devil and the Deep BLUE Sea, Cab Calloway; BLUE, Joni Mitchell; BLUE Angel, Roy Orbison; BLUE Bayou, Roy Orbison; BLUE Collar, Bachman Turner Overdrive; BLUE Eyes, Elton John; BLUE Eyes Crying in the Rain, Willie Nelson; BLUE Hawaii, Elvis Presley; BLUE Jean, David Bowie; BLUE Monday, Fats Domino; BLUE Money, Van Morrison; BLUE Moon, Billie Holiday; BLUE Moon of Kentucky, Bill Monroe; BLUE Morning, BLUE Day, Foreigner; BLUE on BLUE, Bobby Vinton; BLUE Skies, Benny Goodman; BLUE Sky, Allman Brothers Band; BLUE Sky Mine, Midnight Oil; BLUE Train, John Coltrane; BLUE Turns to Grey, Rolling Stones; BLUE Velvet, Bobby Vinton; BLUEberry Hill, Fats Domino; BLUEbird, Paul McCartney; Brown to BLUE, Elvis Costello; Bullet the BLUE Sky, U2; California BLUE, Herb Alpert; Computer BLUE, Prince (or The Artist Formerly Known as); Crystal BLUE Persuasion, Tommy James and the Shondells; Deacon BLUEs, Steely Dan; Devil with a BLUE Dress On, Mitch Ryder; Don't It Make Your Brown Eyes BLUE, Crystal Gayle; Dream of the BLUE Turtles, Sting; For You BLUE, Beatles; Forever in BLUE Jeans, Neil Diamond; It's All Over Now, Baby BLUE, Bob Dylan; Jackie BLUE, Ozark Mountain Daredevils; Midnight BLUE, Electric Light Orchestra; My BLUE Heaven, Artie Shaw; New BLUE Moon, Traveling Wilburys; Old BLUE, Byrds; Out of the BLUE, The Band; Pink Cocktail for a BLUE Lady, Glenn Miller; Pink Turns to BLUE, Husker Dü; Red Roses for a BLUE Lady, Andy Williams; Rednecks, White Socks, and BLUE Ribbon Beer, Johnny Russell; Rhapsody in BLUE, George Gershwin; Runnin BLUE, The Doors; Silver, BLUE and Gold, Bad Company; Song Sung BLUE, Neil Diamond; Stella BLUE, Grateful Dead; Stone BLUE, Foghat; Suite: Judy BLUE Eyes, Crosby, Stills & Nash; Tangled Up in BLUE, Bob Dylan; True BLUE, Madonna

Blue Moons

You may have heard someone say that something happens only "once in a blue moon."

But just what is a blue moon and why do people measure time by it? Well, first things first:

A blue moon isn't blue. Nope. Instead, a blue moon is a term for the second full moon to occur in one calendar month.

For instance, in June 1996, there was a full moon on June 1 and then a second full moon on June 30.

That's a pretty rare thing. Most of the time there's only one full moon in each calendar month.

So, just how rare is "once in a blue moon"? Well, astronomers say blue moons—two full moons in one calendar month—actually occur about every two and a half years.

While you wait...

You might want to learn to sing the song "Blue Moon." It's a famous song written by Lorenz Hart and Richard Rogers about someone waiting for love to find them.

Official Blue Moon Club

No one knows how the term "blue moon" got invented to describe two full moons in a single month. But people use it now to describe something that does not happen very often. Like, "It's only once in a blue moon that we don't get homework in math class."

Use the space on the right to write in your nominees for the Blue Moon Club—things that you think won't happen again for a long time. It could be about you ("It will be a blue moon before I eat another pickle and ice cream sandwich"), or about something else ("It will be a blue moon before the Chicago Cubs win the World Series").

45

It will be a blue moon before...

1.

2.

3.

4.

5.

6.

7.

8.

9.

10.

46

Blue Moons over Blue Waters

Speaking of moons, did you ever wonder why so many toilet bowls hold blue water? (Is it because they're supposed to taste minty fresh?) Honestly, it is pretty weird. So why are they blue? Well, wonder no more. Because after a super special *Blue Book* Investigation, we've solved the mystery for you.

The blue water in toilets comes from toilet soaps such as 2,000 Flushes that are used to clean and deodorize toilets. We'll let Dean Siegal, a spokesperson for 2,000 Flushes, tell you why they use the color blue: "In all consumer products, blue means clean. Whenever people are asked what color means 'clean,' they say blue."

Got it ?

Flush with Activity

But a lot of work goes into that blue color and making sure it works and stays blue for, well, 2,000 flushes. The company has a special lab with 76 toilets where they test 2,000 Flushes under different flushing patterns, like "the morning rush," "the night-time lull," and "the two-week vacation."

Blue Light (That's Not from a Blue Moon)

You might be able to buy 2,000 Flushes at Kmart as a "blue light special"—those 15-minute long sales that are identified by a flashing blue light in the aisle that lets shoppers know where to find the bargain. The blue light special was invented in 1965 by Earl Bartell, an assistant manager of a Kmart in Michigan, as a way to get people excited about sales. He attached an old police car light to a pole and moved it around the store.

Big Blue

Other companies like blue, too. Maybe that's because they want to be blue chip companies. On Wall Street, stocks of companies that are good investments are called "blue chip stocks." The phrase "blue chip" refers to the chip with the highest value in poker. Since poker, like Wall Street, is all about taking chances, it's only fitting that they use this term.

One company that's long been a blue chip company is IBM (International Business Machines). In fact, its nickname is "Big Blue." The name comes from the color of the big mainframe computers (this was in the days before desktop computers) that the company sold in the 1960s. These computers were blue and as big as a classroom. So you can see why they got the name Big Blue.

YOUR MOVE But Big Blue is also the brains behind Deep Blue. What's Deep Blue? It's the world's most accomplished chess computer. In February 1996, Garry Kasparov, the world chess champion, played a seven-game match against Deep Blue and won, 4–2. That's right, the computer won two games against the world's best chess brain. In April 1997 they had a rematch, and Deep Blue won, 3.5–2.5. (Maybe that's because Deep Blue can analyze 200 million moves per second, while even a genius human like Kasparov can only analyze two moves per second.) Deep Blue is at the leading edge of artificial intelligence.

Blue Food

Not Eggs-actly

Nature gave eggs whites, not blues, but when it comes to Easter eggs, white isn't all it's cracked up to be. According to a recent poll, American's favorite Easter egg color is blue.

We Found Our Thrill

Blueberries are native to North America. But it was not until 1906 that people started to cultivate blueberry bushes on blueberry farms. Until then, people just ate blueberries off of wild bushes. The first commercial shipments of blueberries were made in 1916. Now blueberries are a billion-dollar industry.

Yummy for the Tummy

Did someone say "minty fresh" a minute ago? Is anyone else around here hungry? Well, don't bother looking for any blue food. Because there are no truly blue foods. Nope. Scientists say that the fact is, there isn't a natural blue pigment in food. So, if a food appears to be blue it's because it has pigments of red or purple in it (either that, or it's been artificially created). Even blueberries are more purplish than blue.

Scientists say that, for humans, the color blue is actually an appetite suppressant. That means that it makes you not want to eat as much. So the color blue is associated with eating less. This is why many food marketers use it in the packaging of low-calorie foods such as club soda, skim milk, and cottage cheese. (Take a look at these products and see.) People actually eat less when their food is on a blue plate. And if you put a blue light bulb inside your refrigerator, you'll also eat less because the food looks unappetizing. If you really want not to eat, put a blue light bulb over your dinner table. (Your food might not look so good, but maybe your whole family will finally look better.)

There are lots of companies that make blue dyes for use in products like candy. They have names such as Triphenylmethane, Chromium Hydroxide, and FD&C Green #1. The weird thing is, some of these dyes start as a powder that's not blue; they turn blue only when water is added.

A Tan that Faded

In January 1995, candy fans were offered the opportunity to vote for a new M&Ms color. The choices were pink, purple, blue, or no change. Blue won with more than 54 percent of the votes and became an official M&M color in September 1995. The bad news: To make room in the bag for blue, tan M&Ms were retired.

Did You Cut Some?

The blue in blue cheese is actually veins of mold. Some of the kinds of blue cheese are: Roquefort, Stilton, Gorgonzola, Bleu de Bresse, Pipo Crem, Danablu, American Blue. (You can also have blue cheese dressing on your green salad.)

THE BLUE PLATE SPECIAL

If all this talk about food has made you hungry, maybe it's time for a blue plate special. A blue plate special is what restaurants call the special dish of the day. It got that name because it used to be served on a blue plate (they didn't know back then that blue made you less hungry).

★ BLUE PLATE SPECIAL ★

BLUEberry pancakes, BLUEberry syrup, Scram-BLUEd eggs, BLUE milk, BLUE sports drink, BLUE corn chips, turkey sandwich with BLUE mayonnaise and

WE CALL IT CORN

Blue cornmeal, which is used in chips and tortillas, is made from corn that is purple, which grows primarily in New Mexico.

50

Can I Have Seconds?

Blue Food for You

We've cooked up a real blue plate special: an entire day's worth of blue food. (Note: most of these foods can be turned blue just by adding some blue food coloring. Be sure you get the chef's permission before you do it. Otherwise, you might go hungry.)

WHAT A PROJECT
Pepsi Cola likes the color blue so much it started a special $500 million project code-named "Project Blue." The project calls for changing the design of all its cans and signs all over the world to electric blue by 1998.

BLUE ice pop, BLUE mashed potatoes, BLUE cheeseburger, BLUE macaroni & cheese, BLUE point oysters, BLUE Jell-o, BLUE cheese

BLUE PLATE SPECIAL

Bluems

Tiptoe Through the Blulips

Well, you can't eat them, but having them on a table sure makes for a nice meal. We're talking about flowers. Blue flowers and plants. Blue blooms.

As flowers go, blue is one of the rarest colors. Scientists think this has to do with pollination and bees.

(Doesn't everything go back to the birds and the bees?) Bees see only red and yellow. So they visit only red and yellow flowers.

But Mother Nature did do one good thing with blue flowers: They often have the strongest fragrance. And that's what attracts some other insects—and a few humans —to them, so the plants do get pollinated.

How many blue flowers are there? Delphiniums, Hydrangeas, Scillia, Hyacinths, Sweet Peas, and Cornflowers are the few that grow in gardens.

There are some blue wildflowers, like Bluebells. And the Bluebonnet is a flower in the pea family. (It's also the state flower of Texas.)

And grass isn't a flower, but Kentucky Blue Grass is a plant. It's the most popular kind of lawn grass in America. It's not actually blue, but the first settlers to Kentucky thought that it looked sort of gray, so they called it blue grass. (It's been a lawn time since any-one questioned this name.)

Roses are red, Violets are blue, actually Violets are violet. But Delphiniums are blue. So are Scilla, and Hydrangeas,

Cornflowers

Sweet Peas

Bluebonnet

Hyacinths

Scilla

Blue Poetry

In flowers, everyone knows that "roses are red, violets are blue..."

But do you know where that poem comes from?

It was written by Edmund Spenser, one of England's greatest poets. He lived from 1552–1599 and wrote one of the most important poems of all time, *The Faerie Queen*, in 1590. It's a poem to Queen Elizabeth. It includes the line,

"Roses red and violets blew,
And all the sweetest flowres,
that in the forest grew."

Hyacinths, Bluebells, Sweet Peas, Cornflowers, and Bluebonnets too.

Hydrangeas

Delphiniums

Bluebell

POETIC LICENSE

You've probably heard this as the more well-known "Roses are red, violets are blue." Well, now it's time to finish the rhyme. (After all, you may be a poet, and you don't even know it.)

Fill in your top three endings for the famous rhyme.

1. Roses are red, violets are blue...

_____

_____

2. Roses are red, violets are blue...

_____

_____

3. Roses are red, violets are blue...

_____

_____

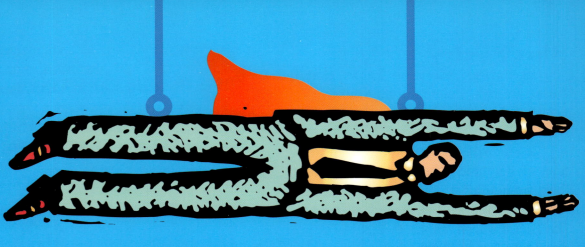

I f you write a good story, someone might want to turn it into a movie. And maybe the movie maker would put some cool special effects in it. Lots of special effects in movies involve the blue screen.

What's a Blue Screen?

Blue screens are what an actor is filmed in front of when the movie maker wants to add a special effect. Blue is used because it contrasts well with flesh and so it's easy to see what's happening. Anyway, say you want to show Superman flying through the air. Well, the movie maker attaches Superman to wires and hangs him from the ceiling so he looks like he's flying. Then he's filmed in front of the blue background.

Later, through the magic of special effects, (and a machine called an "optical printer" that combines two different pieces of movie film—in this case, Superman hanging from a ceiling, and footage of a city as seen from someone flying over the city in a plane) a background of city building tops replaces the blank blue background, and the wires are removed. Thus, Superman appears to be flying.

Blue Films

Blues in the Night, Almost Blue, The Blue Beast, The Blue Bird, Beyond the Blue Horizon, Blue Hawaii, The Blue Veil. Not to mention three movies just titled *Blue* in one of which had you stare at a blank blue screen and listen to the actors

Blue Jeans

Next time you go to the movies, you might want to wear something blue. Starting with everyone's favorite blue, blue jeans. Blue jeans were invented by Levi Strauss in 1873. They were first popular with gold miners in the American West because unlike most pants they were very sturdy and didn't rip or tear or wear out. Since the miners crawled around a lot on rocks and all, that was important.

The word "jeans" comes from the French word for "Genoa," a town in Italy (French and Italian . . . sounds like salad dressing!)—where the sailors were known for their stiff sturdy work pants (but they weren't blue jeans).

Blue jeans are made from denim, a cotton fabric that has white and blue threads. Denim was invented in Nimes, France, and was called "Serge de Nimes" (Cloth of Nimes); people shortened it to "de Nimes," which became "denim." Levi Strauss invented jeans when he took some denim material that was used for tents and made a pair of pants from it.

For every five pairs of jeans made, there's a pound of scrap denim left over from the trimming and cutting. That adds up to 85,000 tons of denim scrap each year. All that scrap used to be scrapped—thrown in land fills or burned. But scientists have figured out a way to recycle the scrap, turning it into pencils and stationery.

Old Lady Blue

Eye Makeup

Nail Polish

Blue Bowling Ball (optional)

Jewelry

Blue Polyester

Blue Jeans

Blue Suede Shoes

DRESS BLUE If you eat enough blue food, you might turn blue from head to toe (like the girl in *Willy Wonka and the Chocolate Factory* who turned into a giant blueberry). Well, probably not. But there are enough blue clothes in the world that you could dress from head to toe in blue. Just look at this.

57

Try this on, too'...

MORE BLUE CLOTHES

Here Comes the Bride

Most brides wear white on their wedding day. But most wear a bit of blue because of the old saying about what a bride should wear:

Something old, Something new, Something borrowed, Something blue...

The importance of blue in weddings goes back to biblical times, when blue represented loyalty and faith.

With This Box, I Thee Wed

...And before most people get married, they get engaged with a ring. Tiffany and Co. is a very famous jewelry store. Its rings all come in boxes that are robin's-egg blue.

TIFFANY & Co.

We See London . . .

Whatever you decide to wear that's blue, don't forget your *bloo*mers. Bloomers are a kind of leggings invented for women in the 1800s by Amelia Bloomer. They were worn under a dress. These days, "bloomers" means any kind of underwear.

Is Blue a Boy Color?

Baby boys are traditionally dressed in blue. (Girls are dressed in pink.) Maybe if the adults asked the babies if they really liked these colors, things would change. "Mother, I would like to wear my lime floral diaper with the matching hat today." But when was the last time you saw an adult who was interested in what a kid had to say?

Blue-niforms

When it comes to clothing, your everyday uniform might involve blue jeans. But some people wear blue all the time. It's part of their blue-niform (we mean uniform). Like sailors. They of course wear navy blue. The United States Navy wears blue uniforms because blue is the color of the ocean. The color "navy blue" is a deep dark blue.

But it's not just the Navy that has blue uniforms. Every branch of the United States military (the Army, Air Force, Navy, Marines, and Coast Guard) has a "dress blue" uniform. Dress blues are their formal uniform (what they have to wear for fancy occasions). They wear dress blues in the winter and dress whites in the summer.

Before you run off and enlist to get your blue uniform, try checking into becoming a cub scout first. They too wear a uniform of blue.

The Fashion Police

Police officers have blue uniforms, too. No one knows exactly why police uniforms are blue, however. But it probably goes back to when police departments began in Europe in the 1700s. Up until then, armies patrolled cities and towns. At first, these new police did not have uniforms. But they began to need something to set them apart from townspeople and soldiers. It is believed that blue was chosen because it was very different from the red uniforms most armies of the time wore. Police departments in America continued the look.

Two hundred years seems like a long time to wear the same thing. Maybe it's time for an update— may we suggest hats with plastic fruit on them?

BLUE FLU

When police officers go on strike (that means they don't report to work because they want more money), they are said to have the "blue flu." In most cities, it's against the law for police to go on strike. So instead of actually going on strike, the police call in and say they're sick. They say they have "the blue flu."

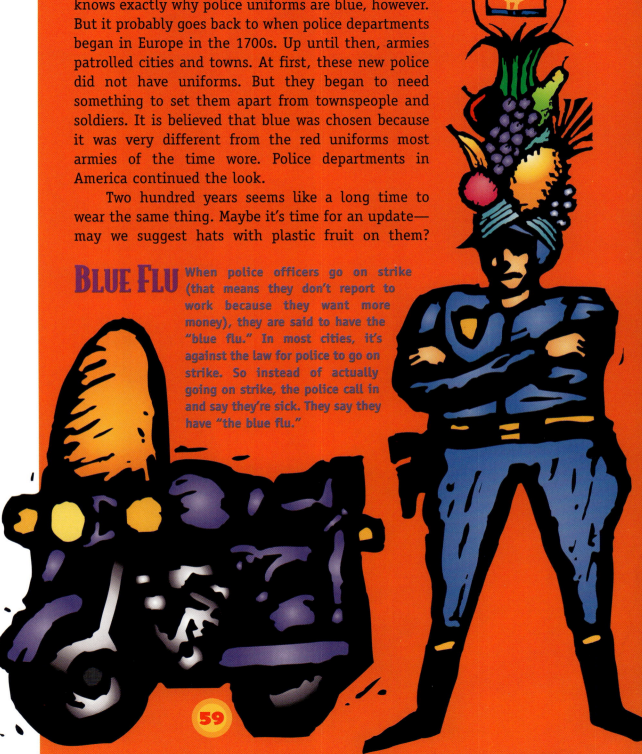

Blue Sports

Every sports team has a uniform. And blue is a big part of sports. Starting with names. Lots of college teams have blue in their name:

There are **Blue Jay** teams at: Creighton, Elmhurst College, Tabor College, Westminster College. Virginia Wesleyan has the **Blue Marlins**, Depaul and Dillard have the **Blue Demons**, Dickinson State has the **Blue Hawks**, Presbyterian College has the **Blue Hose**, Lincoln University has the **Blue Tigers**, Middle Tennessee State has the **Blue Raiders**, Illinois College has the **Blue Boys**, John Carroll has the **Blue Streaks**, the University of Delaware has the Fightin' **Blue Hens**, Milliken has **Big Blue**, Livingstone College has the Fighting **Blue Bears**.

There are **Blue Devil** teams at: Duke, Central Connecticut State, Lawrence Technical University, the State University of New York at Fredonia, and the University of Wisconsin at Stout.

What would you name your team if it were blue?

60

STATES OF A FEATHER

Delaware is known as the Blue Hen State. That's because its regiment in the Revolutionary War was known as the Game Cock Regiment, due to its feistiness. Its commander, Captain Caldwell, believed the best fighting cocks were born from blue hens. So, the Delaware warriors became known as the Blue Hen's Chickens. And Delaware became known as the Blue Hen State.

In pro baseball, there are the Toronto **Blue Jays**.

And **Vida Blue** was a pitcher in the majors from 1969–1986. He helped the Oakland A's to win the World Series in 1972 and 1973.

In hockey, there's the **St. Louis Blues**. And don't forget the New York Rangers, who are known to their fans as the "Blue Jerseys" because of their uniforms. Speaking of hockey, don't forget the blue lines. Hockey rinks have two blue lines on them. These lines, one near each net, divide the rink into three parts: the "defending zone," which is the area near one goal; the "neutral zone," which is the middle of the rink; and the "attacking zone," which is the area near the other goal.

And remember: If you like to watch professional wrestling, you like watching the blue-collar ballet.

BLUE COLLAR

Lots of people are known as "blue collar workers." Blue collar workers are people who work jobs that generally don't involve getting dressed up in a suit (those are "white collar" jobs) such as mechanics or truck drivers. The term comes from the blue workshirts these people generally wear.

In archery, the second ring from the center bull's-eye is blue.

Blue Laws

Maybe it's only right that police have blue uniforms. That way, they can enforce blue laws.

What's a blue law? Well, it's not a law against farting. (Don't you wish that there were one? Then again, maybe you don't. Or you might be Public Enemy Number One and be spending a lot of time in prison.) Blue laws generally forbid all work or play on Sunday. (They are called blue laws because the

Four states don't allow dancing on Sunday. Pennsylvania doesn't allow you to buy meat on Sunday.

Not for sale today! Come back tomorrow.

Puritans—who were a very strict American religious group (remember them? "the bluenoses")—created the American laws during the Colonial period and wrote the laws in books bound in blue paper.) During Colonial times, you could be fined for cooking or even making a bed on Sunday. The first blue law passed on American soil was in the colony of Virginia in 1610 and said that if a person missed church three times in a row, he should be put to death.

Even our first President George Washington was subject to blue laws. Just after he was elected president, he was riding in his carriage from Connecticut to New York to attend church on a Sunday. He was stopped, however, because Connecticut had a law forbidding anyone from traveling on Sunday. In fact Connecticut had so many

blue laws it once was known as the Blue Law State.

Over the years, blue laws have re-mained in effect but they have gotten a bit less harsh. And a bit goofier. As of recently, it was illegal to get your hair cut on Sunday in 10 states because barber shops had to stay closed.

Maine and South Carolina say it is illegal for movie theaters to be open. In Illinois, it's illegal to buy a car.

NO SALE TODAY

63

WHEW! We hope this book hit a bull's-eye with you. We feel like we've talked a blue streak (that means talking fast about something) on blue. Thanks for reading us, We hope we blue you away! If not, throw this book in a blue recycling bin.

More Bluetiful Books from Planet Dexter

ANIMAL GROSSOLOGY™
The Science of All Creatures Gross and Disgusting
by Sylvia Branzei

The author of Planet Dexter's best-selling *Grossology* returns, with this often stomach-turning book about animal life. Find out how a fly eats (yikes!), how to learn from an owl pellet, why a hagfish is so slimy, what the deal is with leeches, and much more.

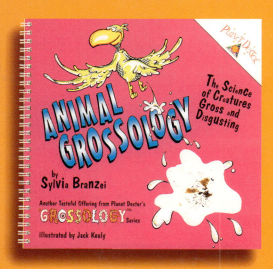

THE HAIRY BOOK
The (Uncut) Truth About the Weirdness of Hair
by The Editors of Planet Dexter

Think you know hair? Think again! This hair-covered book gives you the real scoop on everything from blue-haired dogs to werewolves, wacky styles, and hairy babies. Includes a truly stylin' comb for proper book grooming.

WHADDAYA DOIN' IN THERE?
A Bathroom Companion (for Kids!)
by The Editors of Planet Dexter

All smart kids read in the bathroom. But what to read? Answer: This book, if you can! *Whaddaya Doin' In There?* offers humor, bathroom lore, ghost stories, weird laws, lotsa trivia, you name it. It's the perfect tome for your toilet time. And it comes with a pine-scented air freshener!

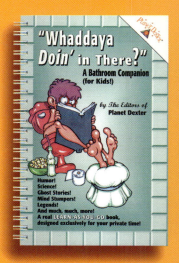